# BATTLEFIELD OF THE MIND
## STUDY GUIDE

Winning the Battle in Your Mind
Revised Edition

JOYCE MEYER

Faith
Words

NEW YORK · NASHVILLE

FaithWords

Hachette Book Group

1290 Avenue of the Americas, New York, NY 10104

faithwords.com

twitter.com/faithwords

Originally published in trade paperback by FaithWords in October 2002.

Revised Edition: January 2018.

FaithWords is a division of Hachette Book Group, Inc.
The FaithWords name and logo are trademarks of Hachette Book Group, Inc.

The publisher is not responsible for websites (or their content) that are not owned by the publisher.

The Hachette Speakers Bureau provides a wide range of authors for speaking events. To find out more, go to www.hachettespeakersbureau.com or call (866) 376-6591.

ISBN: 978-1-5460-3330-1

Printed in the United States of America

LSC-C

Printing 7, 2021

# CONTENTS

The purpose of this study guide is to reinforce the principles taught in my book, *Battlefield of the Mind*. You will need a copy of *Battlefield of the Mind* to work through this book.

This study guide is written in a question and answer format and it also provides space for you to reflect on the lesson and apply the principles to your life. By reading a chapter in *Battlefield of the Mind*, the designated Scripture verses, then answering the questions in the corresponding chapter of the study guide, you will gain a deeper understanding of the principles and learn more easily how to incorporate them into your daily life.

To use this study guide, first read the corresponding chapter in *Battlefield of the Mind*. Next, look up the scriptures designated in the study guide and read them in your Bible. This is an important step because those scriptures are the basis of the teaching in that particular chapter and are taken directly from that chapter.

Answer the questions in the study guide by referring to the appropriate chapter in *Battlefield of the Mind* and your own life.

1. Work at a comfortable pace. Don't rush to finish quickly. Stay in each chapter until you have a thorough understanding of the material and how it pertains to your life.
2. Follow these steps with each chapter in this study guide.
3. Use this study guide for individual study or group discussion. When using it in a group, discuss your answers and learn how to apply the

principles in a way that may not have occurred to you until you heard the experiences of others.

Each chapter in the study guide includes the following sections:

- **Get Ready**: Gets you ready to read the opening verses and section of the book. In some chapters, this section is also where you can reflect on what you've done from the previous chapter and assess how your mind has changed.
- **Get Set**: This section gets more into the "meat" of the chapter and pushes you to further understand the principles.
- **Go to Battle**: This section is a call to action, where you are asked to reflect on ways you can practice the principles and apply them to your everyday life.
- **Remember**: The final section in each chapter gives you a main point from the chapter and a scripture. It's a good idea to write down these short sayings and scriptures on index cards to refer to them quickly. You may also want to memorize those you especially need to apply to your thinking.

Consistently and steadily working through this book will help you renew your mind to God's Word. You will find that your pattern of thinking is gradually transforming from wrong, negative thoughts into God-like thoughts. Changing your way of thinking will enable you to change things in your life that you thought you would have to live with forever.

## WALK IN GOD'S GOOD PLAN FOR YOU

Lining up our thoughts with God's thoughts is vital to overcoming negative thoughts from Satan and brings freedom and peace. We must know God's Word well enough to be able to compare what is in our mind with what is in the mind of God; any thought that attempts to exalt itself above the Word of God we are to cast down and bring into captivity to Jesus Christ. This process takes time. I believe the God-directed, God-empowered principles in this study guide are important tools that will help you achieve this goal. I want to encourage you to study and meditate on them; then apply what you learn to your life and allow the Holy Spirit to enlighten the eyes of your spirit (which is your heart) with God's wisdom and revelation. As you do, I believe you will see great results in winning the war that Satan has launched and ensure your victory in the battlefield of your mind.

If you are one of millions of people who suffer from worry, doubt, confusion, depression, anger or condemnation, you are experiencing an attack in your mind. But you don't have to live your whole life like this! Satan offers wrong thinking to everyone, but you do not have to accept his offer.

I pray that working through this study guide, along with the book, *Battlefield of the Mind*, will help firmly establish in your heart forever that you need to begin to think about what you are thinking about, so that you line up your thoughts with God's thoughts. This renewal of the mind is a process that requires time, but it is well worth the effort.

# BATTLEFIELD OF THE MIND
## STUDY GUIDE

# PART I

# The Importance of the Mind

# Introduction

It is easy to read and contains one of the foundational truths that we must have in order to access the new life we are offered through our relationship with Christ.

The Bible makes it clear that the mind is the leader or forerunner of all actions. Proverbs 23:7 tells us: *For as he* [a person] *thinks in his heart, so is he....* (Also see Romans 8:5.) If we renew our mind according to God's Word, we will, as Romans 12:2 promises, prove for ourselves "what is the good and acceptable and perfect will of God" for our lives. If we think and dwell on negative thoughts, we will have a negative life.

God wants us to experience the fullness of life He sent Jesus to provide for all those who believe in Him and receive it; Satan wants to stop us from receiving all that God has for us. Because our actions are a direct result of our thoughts, Satan's strategy is to wage war against us in our minds by bombarding us with thoughts contrary to the truth of God's Word. He wants to deceive us into believing damaging patterns of untrue thoughts, or strongholds, that we will allow to influence our lives and hold us in bondage.

The battlefield is the mind, and 2 Corinthians 10:4-5 describes the weapons of warfare God has given us "for the overthrow and destruction of strongholds." This study guide describes how to use those weapons. When you begin to see God's good plan for you in your thinking, you will begin to walk in it.

1. Read 2 Corinthians 10:4-5; Proverbs 23:7 KJV.

   Why are our thoughts important?

   _____

   _____

   _____

   _____

2. Read Romans 8:5.

   How do our actions relate to our thoughts?

   _____

   _____

   _____

   _____

3. Read Romans 12:2.

   How will our lives be changed if we renew our minds according to God's Word?

   _____

   _____

   _____

   _____

4. Review 2 Corinthians 10:4-5.

   How will we know the difference between what is in our mind and what is the mind of God?

   _____

   _____

   _____

   _____

# The Mind Is a Battlefield

*Before you begin, read Chapter 1 in* Battlefield of the Mind.

Spend a few moments writing, reflecting on messages that stood out for you in the chapter. Write your thoughts below.

_____

_____

_____

_____

## Get Ready!

Read the scriptures that open Chapter 1: Ephesians 6:12 and John 8:44 from several versions of the Bible. Then answer the questions:

How does Satan attempt to defeat us?

_____

_____

What did Jesus call the devil?

_____

_____

_____

[The devil] knows what we like and what we don't like. He knows our insecurities, our weaknesses, and our fears. He knows what bothers us most. He is willing to invest any amount of time it takes to defeat us. One of the devil's strong points is patience. (page 7)

In what way does Satan try to bombard our minds to defeat us?

_____

_____

_____

Explain the phrase: "One of the devil's strong points is patience."

_____

_____

_____

Read 2 Corinthians 10:4-5.

What are "strongholds," and how does Satan attempt to set them up in our mind?

_____

_____

_____

## Get Set!

Read the examples of strongholds Mary and John encountered on pages 9-14 and give an example of a stronghold you have struggled with in your life.

_____

_____

_____

How might this stronghold you have struggled with have come about?

_____

_____

Read John 8:31-32; Mark 4:24.
How can we overcome strongholds?

_____

_____

How are we to use the weapon of the Word of God to overcome strongholds?

_____

_____

Why are prayer and praise effective weapons in overcoming strongholds?

_____

_____

_____

What are other ways you can defeat strongholds?

_____

_____

_____

The truth is always revealed through the Word; but sadly, people don't always accept it. It is a painful process to face our faults and deal with them. Generally speaking, people justify misbehavior. They allow their past and how they were raised to negatively affect the rest of their lives.

Our past may explain why we're suffering, but we must not use it as an excuse to stay in bondage.

Everyone is without excuse because Jesus always stands ready to fulfill His promise to set the captives free. He will walk us across the finish line of victory in any area if we are willing to go all the way through it with Him. (page 15)

According to this passage, what has God promised concerning the poor, the captives, the blind, the oppressed and others?

_____

_____

## Go to Battle

God never loses a battle. He has a definite battle plan—and when we follow it, we always win! Praise and worship are really battle positions! They confuse the enemy. When we take our position, we will see the enemy's defeat!

Read Luke 4:18-19.

According to this passage what has God promised to the poor, the captive, the blind, the oppressed, and the others?

_____

_____

_____

What can John and Mary (in the text) do that will set them free from their conflicting problems?

_____

_____

_____

Read 1 Corinthians 10:13.

What does this verse say about God and the temptations and trials we encounter when tearing down strongholds?

_____

_____

_____

_____

## Remember

There is a war going on, and your mind is the battlefield. But the good news is that God is fighting on your side.

The temptations in your life are no different from what others experience. And God is faithful. He will not allow the temptation to be more than you can stand. When you are tempted, He will show you a way out so that you can endure.

(1 Corinthians 10:13, NLT)

CHAPTER 2

# A Vital Necessity

*Before you begin, read Chapter 2 in* Battlefield of the Mind.

## Get Ready!

Read the opening scripture, Proverbs 23:7, aloud. What does this scripture mean to you?

_____

_____

_____

Do you agree with the statement: You cannot have a positive life and a negative mind? Explain why you agree or disagree.

_____

_____

_____

_____

Read Romans 8:5.

To have a successful Christian life, what alternative to fleshly, wrong and negative thoughts is a vital necessity?

_____

_____

_____

If your life is in a state of chaos because of years of wrong thinking, what can you do to straighten it out?

_____

_____

_____

Your life may be in a state of chaos because of years of wrong thinking. If so, it is important for you to come to grips with the fact that your life will not get straightened out until your mind does. You should consider this area one of vital necessity. Be serious about tearing down the strongholds Satan has built in your mind. Use your weapons of the Word, praise, and prayer. (page 20)

## Get Set!

Read Zechariah 4:6.
Since determination is not enough to be set free from strongholds, what else is needed?

_____

_____

In what way is right thinking compared to a heartbeat or blood pressure?

_____

_____

_____

One of the best aids to freedom is asking God for a lot of help—and asking often.

One of your weapons is prayer (asking). You can't overcome your situation by determination alone. You do need to be determined, but determined in the Holy Spirit, not in the effort of your own flesh. The Holy Spirit is your Helper—seek His help. Lean on Him. You can't make it alone. (page 20)

Get in the habit of seeking God's help often to fight the battle in your mind. Write a prayer below.

_____

_____

_____

_____

## Go to Battle

Read Matthew 12:33.

Explain how the phrase "a tree is known by its fruit" pertains to our lives.

_____

_____

_____

Can a person's thought life be discerned by looking at his attitude toward life in general? Explain.

_____

_____

_____

Just as my physical life is dependent upon my vital signs, so my spiritual life is dependent upon spending regular, quality time with God. Once I learned that fellowship with Him is vital, I gave it priority in my life. (page 21)

What will you do to make fellowship with God a priority in your life?

_____

_____

_____

_____

## Remember

Where the mind goes, the man follows.

Not by might, nor by power, but by My Spirit…says the Lord of hosts.

(Zechariah 4:6, paraphrased)

CHAPTER 3

# Don't Give Up!

*Before you begin, read Chapter 3 in* Battlefield of the Mind.

## Get Ready!

What changes have you observed since making time with God a priority? Explain.

_____

_____

_____

Read the opening scripture, Galatians 6:9, and then answer the question.
Why is it important that you do not grow weary and give up?

_____

_____

_____

Read Isaiah 43:2.
What does God promise us regarding difficulties we experience?

_____

_____

_____

Quitting is easy. How can we overcome difficulties?

_____

_____

Write a Bible verse or line from a song that will remind you not to quit when the battle gets hard.

_____

_____

_____

_____

Whatever you may be facing or experiencing right now in your life, I am encouraging you to go through it and not give up!

Habakkuk 3:19 says that the way we develop hind's feet (a hind is an animal that can climb mountains swiftly) is "to walk [not to stand still in terror, but to walk] and make [spiritual] progress upon" the "high places [of trouble, suffering or responsibility]!"

The way God helps us make spiritual progress is by being with us to strengthen and encourage us to "keep on keeping on" in rough times. (page 25)

## Get Set!

Read Deuteronomy 30:19; Proverbs 18:21.

How can we decide what is right or wrong for us on a daily basis?

_____

_____

_____

How can we avoid choosing death?

_____

_____

_____

When we begin to feel that the battle of the mind is just too difficult and that we aren't going to make it, then we must be able to cast down that kind of thinking and choose to think that we are going to make it! Not only must we choose to think that we are going to make it, but we must also decide not to quit. Bombarded with doubts and fears, we must take a stand and say, "I will never give up! God is on my side, He loves me, and He is helping me!" (page 26)

Read Deuteronomy 1:2, 6-8.

Why did it take the Israelites forty years to make an eleven-day journey?

_____

_____

_____

How does their problem relate to us today in our spiritual journey?

_____

_____

_____

## Go to Battle

When God told the Israelites, "You have dwelt long enough on this mountain," what was He really saying?

_____

_____

_____

What is He saying to you today?

_____

_____

_____

Are you ready to leave the "mountain" and move forward in life? Explain what you will do differently.

_____

_____

_____

As we renew our minds with the Word of God, we will begin to see positive changes in our thoughts and in all other areas of life!

Let me urge you to make a quality decision that you are going to get your mind renewed and learn to choose your thoughts carefully. Make up your mind that you will not quit and give up until victory is complete and you have taken possession of your rightful inheritance. (page 28)

## Remember

It's easy to quit; it takes faith to go through.

I call heaven and earth to witness this day against you that I have set before you life and death, the blessings and the curses; therefore choose life, that you and your descendants may live

(Deuteronomy 30:19 AMPC).

# Little by Little

*Before you begin, read Chapter 4 in* Battlefield of the Mind.

## Get Ready

Have you noticed a difference in your thinking now that you've determined not to give up? Explain.

_____

_____

_____

Read the opening scripture Deuteronomy 7:22 and answer the questions.

_____

_____

_____

Why did God tell the Israelites He would clear out their enemies "little by little"?

_____

_____

_____

Why do you think the process of renewing your mind is done little by little also?

_____

_____

_____

What is the "beast" that will consume us if we receive too much freedom too quickly?

_____

_____

_____

## Get Set!

Why do we need to suffer "a little while"? I believe that from the time we actually realize we have a problem until Jesus delivers us, we endure a type of suffering, but we rejoice even more when freedom comes. When we try to do something on our own, fail, and then realize that we must wait on Him, our hearts overflow with thanksgiving and praise as He rises up and does what we can not do ourselves. (page 31)

Read 1 Peter 5:10.

Do you agree with my explanation of why we need to suffer "a little while?" Explain.

_____

_____

_____

Read Romans 8:1.

What can we learn from watching a baby's attempts to walk?

_____

_____

_____

How does the devil try to stop you from renewing your mind?

_____

_____

_____

What can you do to stop his attempts?

_____

_____

_____

Walking after the flesh is

_____

_____

_____

Walking after the Spirit is

_____

_____

_____

When you fail (which you will), that doesn't mean that you are a failure. It simply means that you don't do everything right. We all have to accept the fact that along with strengths we also have weaknesses. Just let Christ be strong in your weaknesses; let Him be your strength on your weak days. (page 32)

## Go to Battle

I refuse to be discouraged. I refuse to be condemned. Father, the Bible says that You don't condemn me. You sent Jesus to die for me. I'll be fine—today will be a great day. You help me choose right thoughts today. (page 33)

Write a plan to overcome condemnation and discouragement, including a verse that will help you.

_____

_____

_____

Write down a verse that can help you.

_____

_____

_____

_____

## Remember

I believe God. I believe He is working in me no matter what I may feel or how the situation may look.

> But let endurance and steadfastness and patience have full play and do a thorough work, so that you may be [people] perfectly and fully developed [with no defects], lacking in nothing
>
> (James 1:4 AMPC).

# Be Positive

*Before you begin, read Chapter 5 in* Battlefield of the Mind.

## Get Ready!

Have you seen a difference in your thoughts little by little? Explain.

_____

_____

_____

Read the verses from the opening scripture (Matthew 8:1-13). Explain the story in your own words.

_____

_____

_____

_____

Why do you think Jesus told the man: "It shall be done for you as you have believed?"

_____

_____

_____

How do Jesus' words apply to us today?

_____

_____

Begin to think positively about your life. Practice being positive in each situation that arises. Even if whatever is taking place in your life at the moment is not so good, expect God to bring good out of it, as He has promised in His Word. (page 38)

## Read Romans 8:28; 12:16

What does the Bible say about "all things" in the verses?

_____

_____

_____

How are we to react when our plans don't work out?

_____

_____

_____

Read 2 Corinthians 5:17.

Many of us have had bad things happen to us, things which cause us to be negative about the future. According to this verse, how should we react to such situations?

_____

_____

_____

Read John 16:7-8.

Why did Jesus say it was "profitable" for us that He go away?

_____

_____

_____

As "a new creation," you don't have to allow the old things that happened to you to keep affecting your new life in Christ. You're a new creature with a new life in Christ. You can have your mind renewed according to the Word of God. Good things are going to happen to you. Rejoice! It's a new day! (page 40)

## Go to Battle

Read Philippians 1:6.

What does Jesus teach us that the Holy Spirit will do for us?

_____

_____

_____

What does the Bible say about the work God has begun in us?

_____

_____

_____

We believe for many things, but beyond them all, we believe in Someone. That Someone is Jesus. We don't always know what is going to happen. We just know it will always work out for our good! The more positive you and I become, the more we will be in the flow of God. God is certainly positive, and to flow with Him, we must also be positive. (page 43)

Read Acts 17:11 KJV.

How can we achieve balance in our thinking?

_____

_____

_____

Read Romans 4:18-20; Hebrews 6:19.

Being positive does not mean that we are to ignore the obvious. How do we deal with impossible situations without losing hope?

_____

_____

What is the anchor of the soul? How does it help us?

_____

_____

_____

Read Isaiah 30:18; Proverbs 15:15.

   What is God's desire toward us according to these verses?

_____

_____

_____

What do we need to do to receive His will for us?

_____

_____

_____

   You may not be able to resist the sin of speaking negatively, but when you do, ask God to help you. Speaking negatively about yourself will hinder the good things God has for you.

Reword the way you've been saying things or thinking about them—even tough situations you are going through.

_____

_____

_____

_____

Read 1 Peter 3:10.

   What does this verse say we must do if we want to enjoy life and see good days?

_____

_____

_____

How will you incorporate this verse into your everyday life and practice speaking positively?

_____

_____

_____

## Remember

Don't ever let evil forebodings hang around in your atmosphere; instead, resist them aggressively in the name of Jesus Christ.

> For let him who wants to enjoy life and see good days [good—whether apparent or not] keep his tongue free from evil and his lips from guile (treachery, deceit)
>
> (1 Peter 3:10 AMPC).

# Mind-Binding Spirits

*Before you begin, read Chapter 6 in* Battlefield of the Mind.

## Get Ready!

How has thinking and speaking positively about your circumstances made a difference for you this week? Explain.

_____

_____

_____

Read the opening scripture Philippians 4: 6-7. How can we experience the peace of God?

_____

_____

_____

Read John 8:31-32; Psalm 107:20.

How can we overcome "mind-binding spirits"?

_____

_____

_____

Pay attention to the condition of your mind and keep it free, peaceful, and full of faith. (page 51)

Take an assessment of your mind. Have you kept it free, peaceful and full of faith? Explain.

_____

_____

_____

_____

## Get Set!

Read Romans 8:26; James 1:2-8.

As Christians, why must we decide to believe? How can we believe during times when our minds don't understand everything?

_____

_____

_____

What should we do when we are going through trials?

_____

_____

_____

The devil never runs out of fiery darts to throw against us when we are trying to go forward. Lift up your shield of faith and remember James 1:2-8 which teaches us that we can ask God for wisdom in trials and He will give it to us and will show us what to do. (from page 52)

Read James 1:2-8 from several versions.

Write down key words that stand out to you.

_____

_____

_____

## Go to Battle

I'm sure that you are reading this book right now because you were led to it. You too may be having problems in this area. If so, I encourage you to pray in Jesus' name. By the power of His blood, come against all evil spirits that hinder godly thoughts. If you feel your mind is sluggish, lazy, and unable to believe, then speak against "mind- binding spirits." Pray this way not just one time but any time you experience difficulty in this area. (page 52)

List any "mind-binding spirits" you are currently experiencing. Then write a prayer asking God to give you wisdom regarding your issue.

_____

_____

_____

_____

_____

Write down any insights you gain from your prayer.

_____

_____

_____

_____

## Remember

Pay attention to the condition of your mind and keep it free, peaceful, and full of faith.

He sent out his word and healed them; he rescued them from the grave.

(Psalm 107:20 NIV).

# Think About What You're Thinking About

*Before you begin, read Chapter 7 in* Battlefield of the Mind.

## Get Ready!

Read the opening scripture Psalm 119:15. What are we to spend our time thinking about or meditating on?

_____

_____

_____

Read Psalm 1:3. What are the benefits of meditation on the Word of God?

_____

_____

_____

Draw a picture of the tree described in Psalm 1:3.

How does this image make you feel?

_____

_____

_____


It is very beneficial to think about God's Word. The more time a person spends meditating on the Word, the more he will reap from the Word. (page 55)


## Get Set!

Read Mark 4:24.

What does this statement tell us: "The more time we spend thinking about the Word we read and hear, the more power and ability we will have to do it—the more revelation knowledge we will have about what we have read or heard"?

_____

_____

_____

Why aren't most Christians living victorious lives?

_____

_____

_____

Read Psalm 1:1-2; Proverbs 4:20.

How do we attend to God's Word?

_____

_____

_____

How does the old saying "practice makes perfect" pertain to Christianity?

_____

_____

Read Joshua 1:8.

"What does this verse say about being successful and prospering?"

_____

_____

_____

How does the devil control people's lives?

_____

_____

_____

Read Ephesians 2:3.

What does the apostle Paul warn us against in this verse?

_____

_____

_____

Why must we think about what we are thinking about?

_____

_____

_____

Read Psalm 48:9; Psalm 143:4-5.

What was King David's response to his feelings of depression and gloom?

_____

_____

_____

How can we overcome feelings of depression and gloom?

_____

_____

_____

Read Romans 12:2.

Why is renewing our minds so vital?

_____

_____

How should we go about renewing our minds according to this verse?

_____

_____

_____

Read Philippians 4:8.

   Why are we instructed to think on good things?

_____

_____

_____

How does Satan deceive people as to the source of their misery?

_____

_____

_____

How can thinking about what you are thinking about help you?

_____

_____

_____

# PART II

# Conditions of the Mind

# Introduction

Have you noticed that the condition of your mind changes? One time you may be calm and peaceful, and another time anxious and worried. Or you may make a decision and be sure about it, then later find your mind in a confused condition concerning the very thing you were previously so clear and certain about.

Because it seems that the mind can be in so many different conditions, it is helpful to know when our minds are normal. That way we can learn to deal with abnormal thinking patterns immediately upon their arrival.

Our minds are not born again with the New Birth experience—they have to be renewed. (Romans 12:2.) Satan will aggressively fight against the renewal of our minds, but it is vital that we press on and continue to pray and study in this area until we gain measurable victory. I believe this next section of the study guide will open your eyes to normal and abnormal mindsets for the believer who has determined to walk in victory.

# When Is My Mind Normal?

*Before you begin, read Chapter 8 in* Battlefield of the Mind.

## Get Ready!

Have you been more mindful of what you have been thinking as a result of reading *Battlefield of the Mind?* Explain.

_____

_____

_____

Read the opening scripture, Ephesians 1:17-18 from several versions of the Bible. Why do you think Paul prays that our hearts will be "flooded with light?"

_____

_____

_____

How can our hearts be flooded with light?

_____

_____

_____

When a person receives Christ as his personal Savior, the Holy Spirit comes to dwell in him. The Bible teaches us that the Holy Spirit knows the mind of God. Just as a person's own spirit within him is the only one who knows his thoughts, so the Spirit of God is the only One Who knows the mind of God. (page 68)

Read 1 Corinthians 2:11.

What comparison can be made between a person's own spirit and the Holy Spirit?

_____

_____

_____

What is one of the purposes of the Holy Spirit?

_____

_____

_____

How is this purpose of the Holy Spirit accomplished?

_____

_____

_____

Why does the Holy Spirit function this way?

_____

_____

_____

## Get Set!

Read 1 Kings 19:11-12 KJV.

How does God speak to us most of the time?

_____

_____

_____

Read 1 Corinthians 14:15.

How did Paul say he prayed?

_____

_____

_____

Read 1 Corinthians 14:13-14.

How does praying in the spirit and interpretation of tongues illustrate the principle of "mind aiding spirit"?

_____

_____

_____

As believers, we are spiritual, and we are also natural. The natural does not always understand the spiritual; therefore, it is vitally necessary for our minds to be enlightened concerning what is going on in our spirits. The Holy Spirit desires to bring us this enlightenment, but the mind often misses what the spirit is attempting to reveal because it is too busy. A mind that is too busy is abnormal. The mind is normal when it is at rest—not blank, but at rest. (page 70)

Describe the difference between a blank mind and a mind at rest.

_____

_____

_____

## Go to Battle

Read the passages that mention speaking in tongues (1 Corinthians 12, 13, 14). Write down any questions you have about speaking in tongues. Discuss them with a trusted spiritual leader or friend.

_____

_____

Praying in the spirit (in an unknown tongue), and interpretation (of that unknown tongue) is a marvelous way to understand the principle of "mind-aiding spirit." The spirit is speaking something, and the mind is given understanding. (page 73)

Read Isaiah 26:3.

Why does the devil want to overload and overwork your mind by filling it with every kind of wrong thought?

_____

_____

_____

What condition should the mind be in?

_____

_____

_____

List 3 ways you will keep your mind at rest.

_____

_____

_____

_____

_____

## Remember

When the mind is stayed on the right things, it will be at rest.

You will keep in perfect peace those whose minds are steadfast, because they trust in you.

(Isaiah 26:3 NIV).

# A Wandering, Wondering Mind

*Before you begin, read Chapter 9 in* Battlefield of the Mind.

## Get Ready!

How have you kept your mind at rest?

_____

_____

_____

Read the opening scripture, 1 Peter 1:13. How can you gird up the loins of your mind?

_____

_____

_____

What does an inability to concentrate indicate?

_____

_____

_____

What are some of the causes of an inability to concentrate?

_____

_____

_____

What is the difference between a lack of comprehension and a lack of concentration?

_____

_____

_____

Many people have spent years allowing their minds to wander because they have never applied principles of discipline to their thought life. (from page 77)

Read 1 Corinthians 2:16.
According to this scripture, what do we as believers "hold" when we have "the mind of Christ"?

_____

_____

_____

Give an example of the kind of mind that should be considered abnormal for a believer.

_____

_____

_____

## Get Set!

If you are like me, you can be sitting in a church service listening to the speaker, really enjoying and benefiting from what is being said, when suddenly your mind begins to wander. After a while you "wake up" to find that you don't remember a thing that has been going on. Even though your body stayed in church, your mind has been at the shopping center browsing through the stores or home in the kitchen cooking dinner.

Remember, in spiritual warfare the mind is the battlefield. That is where the enemy makes his attack. He knows very well that even though a person attends church, if he can't keep his mind on what is being taught, he will gain absolutely nothing by being there. The devil knows that a person cannot discipline himself to complete a project if he cannot discipline his mind and keep it on what he is doing. (page 79)

Read Romans 12:2.

Are our minds reborn with the New Birth experience? Why or why not?

_____

_____

_____

Read 1 Peter 5:7.

Are our minds supposed to wander or be upset, confused, full of doubt and unbelief, or anxious, worried and tormented by fear? Why or why not?

_____

_____

_____

Evaluate your thoughts. How often are you upset or confused? How often are you full of doubt and unbelief? How often are you anxious or worried? Draw a pie chart showing the amount of time your thoughts are: upset/confused; doubtful; worried or anxious; and at rest/peaceful.

## Go to Battle

Read Mark 11: 23-24, NIV and fill in the blanks.

"Truly I tell you, if anyone says to this _____, 'Go, throw yourself into the sea,' and does not _____ in their heart but _____ that what they say will happen, it will be _____ for them. Therefore I tell you, whatever you ask for in prayer, _____ that you have received it, and it will be _____.

What does this verse mean to you especially regarding faith and belief?

_____

_____

_____

_____

What are you believing God for now?

_____

_____

_____

Confess any doubt you may have now and ask God to renew your faith and your mind.

_____

_____

_____

_____

What can you do when doubt creeps into your mind, making your wonder if God hears your prayers or will answer you prayers?

_____

_____

_____

## Remember

Begin today to "keep your foot," to keep your mind on what you're doing. As Christians, as *believers*, we are to believe—not doubt!

> For this reason I am telling you, whatever you ask for in prayer, believe (trust and be confident) that it is granted to you, and you will [get it].
>
> (Mark 11:24 AMPC).

# A Confused Mind

*Before you begin, read Chapter 10 in* Battlefield of the Mind.

## Get Ready!

How have you done with keeping your mind from wandering? What differences have you seen?

_____

_____

_____

_____

Read James 1:5-8. What do you think this scripture means?

_____

_____

_____

Read Matthew 16:8 KJV

    Why are a large percentage of God's people admittedly confused?

_____

_____

_____

What is "reasoning"?

_____

_____

_____

_____

Why shouldn't we rely on reasoning when God directs us to do something?

_____

_____

Reasoning occurs when a person tries to figure out the "why" behind something. Reasoning causes the mind to revolve around and around a situation, issue, or event attempting to understand all its intricate component parts. We are reasoning when we dissect a statement or teaching to see if it is logical, and disregard it if it is not.

Satan frequently steals the will of God from us due to reasoning. The Lord may direct us to do a certain thing, but if it does not make sense—if it is not logical—we may be tempted to disregard it. What God leads a person to do does not always make logical sense to his mind. His spirit may affirm it and his mind reject it, especially if it would be out of the ordinary or unpleasant or if it would require personal sacrifice or discomfort. It is always nice if the spirit and mind agree, but if they don't, we should always choose to follow the spirit. (page 86)

## Get Set!

Read 1 Corinthians 2:14 KJV.

What is the Christian alternative to reasoning in the mind?

_____

_____

Give an example from your own life of a struggle between the carnal mind and the spiritual man.

_____

_____

_____

_____

Read James 1:22.

What are we to do when God speaks to us?

_____

_____

_____

Any time we see what the Word says and refuse to do it, reasoning has somehow gotten involved and deceived us into believing something other than the truth. We cannot spend excessive time trying to understand (mentally) everything the Word says. If we bear witness in the spirit, we can move ahead and do it. (page 89).

Read Proverbs 3:5; Romans 9:1.

Why is excessive reasoning dangerous?

_____

_____

_____

What three things does the human mind like? What is wrong with this?

_____

_____

_____

_____

How did Paul know he was doing the right thing and not relying on his own reasoning?

_____

_____

_____

_____

## Go to Battle

Read 1 Corinthians 2:1-2.

What was Paul's approach to reasoning?

_____

_____

_____

Why is this a good example for us today?

_____

_____

_____


Reasoning is not the normal condition in which God wants our mind to reside.

Be aware that when the mind is filled with reasoning, it is not normal; at least not for the Christian who intends to be victorious—the believer who intends to win the war that is fought on the battlefield of the mind. (page 92)

Do you think you are addicted to reasoning? Explain.

_____

_____

_____

_____

What can you do to depend more on God's spirit than your reasoning?

_____

_____

_____

_____

## Remember

You and I must grow to the place where we are satisfied to know the One Who knows, even if we ourselves do not know.

> Lean on, trust in, and be confident in the Lord with all your heart and mind and do not rely on your own insight or understanding.
>
> (Proverbs 3:5 AMPC).

# A Doubtful and Unbelieving Mind

*Before you begin, read Chapter 11 in* Battlefield of the Mind.

## Get Ready!

Have you experienced more peace of mind now that you've relinquished reasoning? Explain.

_____

_____

_____

Read the verses leading up to the opening scriptures: Matthew 14:22-31 and Mark 6:1-6. Describe what is going on in each set of verses.

_____

_____

_____

_____

What is the difference between the effects of doubt and unbelief?

_____

_____

_____

_____

As we look then at these two powerful tools of the enemy, we see that doubt causes a person to waver between two opinions, whereas unbelief leads to disobedience. (page 95)

## Get Set!

Read 1 Kings 18:21; Romans 12:3 KJV.

How does the devil try to negate our faith?

_____

_____

_____

Why is it so important for us to know the Word of God?

_____

_____

_____

Read Romans 4:18-21.

How did Abraham overcome the attack of Satan?

_____

_____

_____

What tools does Satan use to try to get us to "abort" our dreams?

_____

_____

_____

What do they both work against?

_____

_____

_____

Why does Satan attack us with doubt and unbelief?

_____

_____

Why does the devil not want us to get our mind in agreement with our spirit?

_____

_____

_____

Doubt comes in the form of thoughts that are in opposition to the Word of God. This is why it is so important for us to know the Word of God. If we know the Word, then we can recognize when the devil is lying to us. Be assured that he lies to us in order to steal what Jesus purchased for us through His death and resurrection. (page 96)

## Go to Battle

Look at Matthew 14:24-32; Romans 4:18-21; Ephesians 6:14.

How were Peter and Abraham alike in their faith? How were they different?

_____

_____

_____

_____

What are we to do in times of spiritual warfare?

_____

_____

_____

Why does Satan bring storms into your life?

_____

_____

_____

How do you resist him?

_____

_____

_____

Abraham knew the conditions, but unlike Peter, his circumstances did not seem to hinder his faith. He probably didn't think about them much or talk about them. He kept His mind and conversation on God. You and I can be aware of our circumstances and yet, purposely, keep our mind on something that will build us up and edify our faith. That is why Abraham stayed busy giving praise and glory to God. We glorify God when we continue to do what we know is right even in adverse circumstances. (page 100)

Read James 1:5-7.

Describe a time in your life when you were led by your heart rather than your head.

_____

_____

_____

How can you remember to give praise and glory to God when your circumstances are challenging?

_____

_____

What are some ways you will commit to glorifying God?

_____

_____

## Remember

Since you can choose your own thoughts, when doubt comes you should learn to recognize it for what it is, say "No, thank you"—and keep on believing! The choice is yours!

For therein is the righteousness of God revealed from faith to faith: as it is written, the just shall live by faith.

(Romans 1:17 KJV).

# An Anxious and Worried Mind

*Before you begin, read Chapter 12 in* Battlefield of the Mind.

## Get Ready!

How have you remained focused on God—rather than doubt and unbelief—during challenging circumstances? Explain.

_____

_____

_____

_____

Read Psalm 37:8 from several versions of the Bible. Write down the version that speaks to you the most. Memorize the verse and repeat it every time you are tempted to worry.

_____

_____

_____

_____

Read Galatians 5:22; John 15:4 KJV; Matthew 6:25-34; Philippians 4:6; 1 Peter 5:7.

What are anxiety and worry?

_____

_____

What is peace?

_____

_____

_____

How do we get the peace of God?

_____

_____

_____

Jesus said, "I am the Vine; you are the branches..." (John 15:5.) How long can a branch survive if it is broken off the vine? When we abide in Him, we enter the protection and rest of God. The life of abiding is a peaceful, restful and fruitful life. Enter in and enjoy your life while God works on your problems!

Read Matthew 6:25; John 10:10.
    According to these verses, how is life intended to be?

_____

_____

_____

How does your life compare to John 10:10? What do you think you need to do to live a more fulfilled life?

_____

_____

_____

Why does Satan attack us with worry?

_____

_____

_____

Read Matthew 6:25-30.

What does this passage of Scripture teach us about worry?

_____

_____

_____

## Get Set!

Read Matthew 6:31; 12:34 KJV.

The enemy knows that if he can get enough of the wrong things going on in our mind, what will eventually happen?

_____

_____

_____

Read Matthew 6:32-33.

The world seeks after "things." What are we to seek?

_____

_____

_____

Read Matthew 6:34.

Why shouldn't we spend today worrying about tomorrow?

_____

_____

_____

Read Philippians 4:6; Hebrews 4:12; Ephesians 6:17 KJV.

The Word of God is our sword. Why must it be wielded against the enemy?

_____

_____

_____

How often do you use the sword against the enemy? Describe one time you used it and the results.

_____

_____

_____

_____

_____

In Matthew 6:25 we are being taught that there is nothing in life that we are to worry about—not any aspect of it! The quality of life that God has provided for us is great enough to provide all of the things we need, but if we worry about the things, then we lose them as well as the life He intended us to have. (page 111)

## Go to Battle

Read 2 Corinthians 10:5.

What is the single most effective weapon that can be used to win the war against worry and anxiety?

_____

_____

_____

Read 1 Peter 5:6-7.

Why is a person who worries not a humble person?

_____

_____

_____

What should our first response be in every situation?

_____

_____

_____

Think of a time or a situation you may have worried about in the past. How might you handle that situation differently now that you are seeking to keep your mind and life at peace?

_____

_____

_____

# Remember

Worry certainly never makes anything better, so why not give it up?

And who of you by worrying and being anxious can add one unit of measure (cubit) to his stature or to the span of his life?

(Matthew 6:27 AMPC)

# A Judgmental, Critical and Suspicious Mind

*Before you begin, read Chapter 13 in* Battlefield of the Mind.

## Get Ready!

Have you found yourself worrying less? Explain.

_____

_____

_____

Read Matthew 7:1 KJV.

What does it mean to judge others?

_____

_____

_____

Why is judging others wrong?

_____

_____

_____

Describe a time you felt judged by someone.

_____

_____

_____

_____

Describe a time you judged someone else.

_____

_____

_____

What can you learn from being judged and judging someone else?

_____

_____

_____

God is the only One Who has the right to condemn or sentence, therefore, when we pass judgment on another, we are, in a certain sense, setting ourselves up as God in his life. (page 124)

Read Romans 12:3.

Judgment and criticism are evidence of what deeper problem?

_____

_____

What is the only reason we are able to excel in an area?

_____

_____

How can remembering the reason you are able to excel keep you from judging others?

_____

_____

# Get Set!

Read Galatians 6:1-3.

According to this scripture, what mental attitude are we to maintain within ourselves?

_____

_____

_____

Read Romans 14:4.

How can God help us with our weaknesses?

_____

_____

_____

Is it wrong to have a mental opinion of people?

_____

_____

_____

How can the action of judging and criticizing be changed?

_____

_____

_____

Read Matthew 7:1-2; Galatians 6:7.

How does the principle of sowing and reaping apply to our thoughts?

_____

_____

_____

Read Matthew 7:3-5.

Why does the devil love to keep us busy, mentally judging the faults of others?

_____

_____

How is a judgmental mind an offshoot of a negative mind?

_____

_____

_____

We make excuses for our own behavior, but when someone else does the same thing we do, we are often merciless. Doing unto others as we want them to do to us (see Matt. 7:12) is a good life principle that will prevent a lot of judgment and criticism, if followed.

A judgmental mind is an offshoot of a negative mind—thinking about what is wrong with an individual instead of what is right.

Be positive and not negative! Others will benefit, but you will benefit more than anyone. (page 132)

## Go to Battle

Read 1 Corinthians 13:7.

What is the answer for a judgmental, critical, suspicious mind?

_____

_____

_____

What does it mean to have a "balanced attitude"?

_____

_____

_____

Read John 2:23-25; 1 Peter 5:8; 1 Corinthians 12:10 KJV.

What was Jesus' attitude toward His relationship with others?

_____

_____

_____

Why do we need balance in human relationships?

_____

_____

_____

What is the difference between suspicion and discernment?

_____

_____

_____

What does true spiritual discernment provoke?

_____

_____

_____

Always place your ultimate trust in the Lord. Doing so will open the door for the Holy Spirit to let you know when you're crossing over the line of balance. (page 134)

## Remember

Your actions won't change until your mind does.

Suspicion comes out of the unrenewed mind; discernment comes out of the renewed spirit.

Stay alert! Watch out for your great enemy, the devil. He prowls around like a roaring lion, looking for someone to devour.

(1 Peter 5:8 NLT).

CHAPTER 14

# A Passive Mind

*Before you begin, read Chapter 14 in* Battlefield of the Mind.

## Get Ready!

Have you noticed yourself being less critical, less judgmental and less suspicious of others? Write down what you've noticed and what you'd like to continue to do.

_____

_____

_____

Read Hosea 4:6; 1 Peter 5:8; 2 Timothy 1:6.

What is "passivity" and why is it a dangerous problem?

_____

_____

_____

Why does the devil use passivity?

_____

_____

_____

How can a believer guarantee that the enemy will not win the war?

_____

_____

Passivity is the opposite of activity. It is a dangerous problem because the Word of God clearly teaches that we must be alert, cautious and active (see 1 Pet. 5:8)—that we are to fan the flame and stir up the gift within us (see 2 Tim. 1:6). (page 139)

Read Ephesians 4:27 KJV; Luke 11:24-26.

 Why is it dangerous to give Satan the "empty space" of our mind?

_____

_____

_____

Why doesn't casting down imaginations always work?

_____

_____

_____

_____

## Get Set!

It is impossible to get from wrong behavior to right behavior without *first* changing thoughts. A passive person may want to do the right thing, but he never will do so unless he purposely activates his mind and lines it up with God's Word and will. (page 144)

Read Romans 12:2; John 15:4,10 KJV; Matthew 5:27,28.

 Explain this dynamic principle shown throughout God's Word: "right action follows right thinking."

_____

_____

_____

_____

Fruit comes as the result of what?

_____

_____

What does this involve?

_____

_____

_____

What must a person do to get from wrong behavior to right behavior?

_____

_____

_____

Why is it dangerous to "play around with sin" in the mind?

_____

_____

_____

## Get Set!

Read Colossians 3:1-2.

Explain the phrase, "You must have backbone and not just wishbone!"

_____

_____

_____

What areas of your life do you need to apply this phrase to?

_____

_____

_____

Once again we see the same principle: if you want to live the resurrection life that Jesus has provided, then seek that new, powerful life by setting your mind and keeping it set on things above, not on things on the earth. (page 146)

Take inventory of your thoughts today. Each hour, write down what you spent most of your time thinking about.

_____

_____

_____

_____

_____

_____

## Go to Battle

Review the list of things you spend time thinking about. Which ones do you want to change? What do you want to think about.

_____

_____

_____

_____

You must be active—not passive. Right action begins with right thinking. Don't be passive in your mind. Start today choosing right thoughts. (page 147)

List three or more of your favorite scriptures that you can think about when you find your mind becoming passive or thinking about negative things.

_____

_____

_____

_____

_____

_____

## Remember

If you and I want the good life, then we must keep our mind on good things.

And set your minds and keep them set on what is above (the higher things), not on the things that are on the earth.

(Colossians 3:2 AMPC)

# The Mind of Christ

*Before you begin, read Chapter 15 in* Battlefield of the Mind.

## Get Ready!

What have you been focusing your mind on lately? What differences have you observed in your life?

_____

_____

_____

_____

Read 1 Corinthians 2:16.

    According to this scripture, why is it possible for us to think as Jesus did?

_____

_____

_____

Read Ezekiel 36:26,27; Romans 8:6; Amos 3:3.

    Why did God give us His Spirit—a new nature, a new heart and mind— with the New Birth?

_____

_____

_____

What is the result of following the mind of the flesh? What is the result of following the mind of the Spirit?

_____

_____

_____

What is the first thing we must do in order to flow in the mind of Christ?

_____

_____

_____

What type of outlook and attitude did Jesus display?

_____

_____

_____

The mind of Christ in us is positive; therefore, any time we get negative, we are

_____

_____

_____

What is the dictionary definition of the word "depress"? How does this word apply to us?

_____

_____

_____

We would make tremendous progress simply by learning how to discern life and death. If something is ministering death to you, don't do it any longer. When certain lines of thought fill you full of death (every kind of misery), you know immediately that it is not the mind of the Spirit. (page 152)

## Get Set!

Read Psalm 143:3-10.

What are the eight steps we can take to overcome depression?

_____

_____

_____

_____

_____

Which steps do you need to participate in more readily when negative thoughts fill your mind?

_____

_____

_____

_____

Depression oppresses a person's spiritual freedom and power. Our spirit (empowered and encouraged by God's Spirit) is powerful and free. Therefore, Satan seeks to oppress its power and liberty by filling our mind with darkness and gloom. Please realize that it is vital to resist the feeling called "depression" immediately upon sensing its arrival. The longer it is allowed to remain, the harder it becomes to resist. (page 154)

Read 2 Corinthians 10:4-5; Isaiah 26:3.

Why does Satan use depression?

_____

_____

_____

Where do negative feelings come from?

_____

_____

What is the second thing we must do in order to flow in the mind of Christ?

_____

_____

_____

Read Psalm 63:5,6; 77:12; 119:15; 143:5; 17:15.

If you want to experience victory, what will need to be a regular part of your thought life?

_____

_____

_____

What is the advantage of fellowshipping with God early each morning?

_____

_____

_____

Read John 16:7; Matthew 28:20; Hebrews 13:5; 1 John 4:16.

Since God is always with us, how do we become conscious of His presence?

_____

_____

_____

What is the third thing we must do in order to flow in the mind of Christ?

_____

_____

_____

Review 1 John 4:16 and read Romans 8:35, 37.

How can we experience God's love for us?

_____

_____

_____

What is the result of meditating on and confessing Romans 8:35, 37?

_____

_____

## Go to Battle

Review Psalm 100:4.

What is a sign that a person is flowing in the mind of Christ?

_____

_____

_____

Read Hebrews 13:15; Psalm 34:1.

How can we be a blessing to the Lord?

_____

_____

_____

Why is expressing appreciation so beneficial?

_____

_____

_____

Read Ephesians 5:18-20; John 5:38.

How can we let the Holy Spirit ever fill and stimulate us?

_____

_____

_____

Read Mark 4:22.

Where does the power to do the Word of God come from?

_____

_____

Based on what you learned in this chapter, what will you do more of to keep your mind like Christ's mind?

_____

_____

_____

## Remember

*Think* deliberately according to the Word of God.

Enter into His gates with thanksgiving and a thank offering and into His courts with praise! Be thankful and say so to Him, bless and affectionately praise His name!

(Psalm 100:4)

# PART III

# Wilderness Mentalities

# Introduction

The children of Israel spent forty years in the wilderness making an eleven-day trip because they had a "wilderness mentality." We really shouldn't look at the Israelites with such astonishment because most of us do the same thing they did. We keep going around and around the same mountains instead of making progress. The result is that it takes us years to experience victory over something that could have and should have been dealt with quickly.

A wilderness mentality is a wrong mindset. We can have right or wrong mindsets. The right ones benefit us, and the wrong ones hurt us and hinder our progress. Colossians 3:2 teaches us to set our minds and keep them set. We need our minds set in the right direction because wrong mindsets not only affect our circumstances, but they also affect our inner life.

Read Deuteronomy 1:2.

Why was an eleven-day journey for the children of Israel extended to a forty-year journey?

_____

_____

_____

Read Deuteronomy 1:6.

How are we like the Israelites?

_____

_____

What is God saying to us today that He said to the children of Israel in their day?

_____

_____

_____

Read Colossians 3:2.

What is a wilderness mentality?

_____

_____

_____

What should we do to avoid having a wilderness mentality?

_____

_____

_____

Why do we need our minds set in the right direction?

_____

_____

_____

# Wilderness Mentality #1: "My future is determined by my past and my present"

*Before you begin, read Chapter 16 in* Battlefield of the Mind.

Read Proverbs 29:18 KJV (and the introduction to Section 3).
   What was the Israelites' problem?

_____

_____

_____

Can you relate to the Israelites? Why or why not.

_____

_____

_____

_____

Read Luke 4:18,19 KJV.
   When you face situations that are so bad it seems you have no real reason to hope, what must you remember?

_____

_____

_____

Read Isaiah 11:1-3 KJV.

Can we judge things accurately by the sight of our natural eyes? Why or why not?

_____

_____

_____

Read Numbers 14:2-3.

What was the attitude of the Israelites in this passage?

_____

_____

_____

Read Numbers 20:2-4.

Where do such bad attitudes come from?

_____

_____

_____

Read Numbers 21:4-5.

What other bad attitude of the Israelites do we see evidenced in this passage?

_____

_____

_____

## Get Set!

Read Genesis 13:7-11.

What was Abraham's attitude that allowed him to bless his nephew Lot in order to stay out of strife?

_____

_____

_____

Read Genesis 13:14-15; Romans 4:17 KJV.

What was the result of Abraham's good attitude?

_____

_____

_____

In view of Abraham's situation, how should you think and speak about your future?

_____

_____

_____

Get a new mindset. Believe that with God all things are possible (see Luke 18:27); with man some things may be impossible, but we serve a God Who created everything we see out of nothing (see Heb. 11:3). Give Him your nothingness and watch Him go to work. All He needs is your faith in Him. He needs for you to believe, and He will do the rest. (page 182)

## Go to Battle

Think and speak about your future in a positive way, according to what God has placed in your heart, and not according to what you have seen in the past or are seeing even now in the present. (page 186)

Spend some time meditating on things God has whispered into your spirit about your life and purpose. Write down what you have heard and what you will do going forward to work with God to bring these things into fruition.

_____

_____

_____

## Remember

We need to hear what the Spirit says, not what the world says. Let God speak to you about your future—not everyone else.

> ...(as it is written, "I have made you a father of many nations" in the presence of Him whom he believed—God, who gives life to the dead and calls those things which do not exist as though they did.
>
>                                      (Romans 4:17 NKJV).

# Wilderness Mentality #2: "Someone do it for me; I don't want to take the responsibility."

*Before you begin, read Chapter 17 in* Battlefield of the Mind.

## Get Ready!

Read Genesis 11:31.

How is responsibility often defined?

_____

_____

_____

What does it mean to be responsible?

_____

_____

_____

How did Terah (Abram's father) respond to the opportunity God placed before him?

_____

_____

_____

How are we like Terah? Why do we respond that way?

_____

_____

_____

_____

Read Exodus 32:1-14, 30-32.

For what did the Israelites want to take responsibility? Who did it for them? How?

_____

_____

_____

_____

As a father, what does God want to teach His children?

_____

_____

_____

_____

# Get Set!

Read Proverbs 6:6-11.

Why is it important to be motivated from within, not from without?

_____

_____

_____

Read Matthew 20:16.

In regard to responsibility, the last part of this verse can be interpreted to mean that many are

_____

_____

_____

Read Joshua 1:1-3.

If we are not willing to take our responsibility seriously and go forth to claim our spiritual inheritance, what will be the result?

_____

_____

_____

_____

When God told Joshua that Moses was dead and he was to take his place and lead the people across the Jordan into the Promised Land, it meant a lot of new responsibility for Joshua. The same is true for us as we go forth to claim our spiritual inheritance. You and I will never have the privilege of being used by God if we are not willing to take our responsibility seriously. (page 192)

Read Ecclesiastes 11:4.

How will meeting resistance to your taking responsibility help you?

_____

_____

_____

_____

What will happen if you only do what is easy?

_____

_____

_____

Read Matthew 25:1-13.

According to verse 13 of this passage, what do we need to do while we are waiting for the Master's return?

_____

_____

_____

## Go to Battle

Read Matthew 25:14-28; John 15:16.

How should you respond to the ability that God has placed in you? Why?

_____

_____

_____

_____

What does the Bible clearly show us about God's will for us?

_____

_____

_____

Read 1 Peter 5:6-7 KJV.

What can we learn about care and responsibility from this chapter?

_____

_____

_____

What should you remember if God gives you whatever you ask Him for?

_____

_____

_____

What should anyone operating in the mind of Christ walk in?

_____

_____

_____

Give a two-word summary of this entire chapter.

_____

_____

List two things you will do differently after reading this chapter.

_____

_____

## Remember

The Bible clearly shows us that it is God's will for us to bear good fruit (see John 15:16).

> You didn't choose me. I chose you. I appointed you to go and produce lasting fruit, so that the Father will give you whatever you ask for, using my name.
>
> (John 15:16 NLT).

# Wilderness Mentality #3: "Please make everything easy; I can't take it if things are too hard!"

*Before you begin, read Chapter 18 in* Battlefield of the Mind.

## Get Ready!

Read Deuteronomy 30:11; what do you think the verse means?

_____

_____

_____

_____

Why aren't God's commands too difficult for us?

_____

_____

_____

Read John 14:16.

   When do things get hard?

_____

_____

_____

If everything in life were easy, what effect would it have on our lives?

_____

_____

_____

The Holy Spirit is in us and with us all the time for what purpose?

_____

_____

_____

Read Exodus 13:17; Hebrews 4:16.

If you know God has asked you to do something, what should you do when things get hard?

_____

_____

_____

Why did God lead the children of Israel the long, hard way?

_____

_____

_____

Did entering the Promised Land mean no more battles for the Israelites?

_____

_____

Why did God lead the children of Israel the longer, harder route even though there was a shorter, easier one?

_____

_____

_____

## Get Set!

Things get hard when we are trying to do them independently without leaning on and relying on God's grace. If everything in life were easy, we would not even need the power of the Holy Spirit to help us. The Bible refers to Him as "the Helper." He is in us and with us all the time to help us, to enable us to do what we cannot do—and, I might add, to do with ease what would be hard without Him. (page 200)

Read Galatians 6:9; Luke 4:1-13.

Why is it important that we not give up in the mind, lose heart, grow weary and faint?

_____

_____

_____

_____

How was Jesus' forty-day fast in the wilderness different from the Israelites' forty-year wandering in the wilderness?

_____

_____

_____

Read 1 Peter 4:1-2.

What secret concerning how to make it through difficult things and times does this passage teach us?

_____

_____

_____

## Go to Battle

Read Philippians 4:12-13 AMP; (in addition, read verse 13 in the New King James Version).

What does right thinking do for us?

_____

_____

_____

_____

If you are a whiner and a complainer, what should you do?

_____

_____

What verses can help you remember to lean on God to accomplish His plans for you?

_____

_____

_____

Write a letter to yourself, reminding you to go forth and rely on God to accomplish everything.

_____

_____

_____

_____

_____

Review your letter often.

## Remember

The Holy Spirit tells us not to give up in our mind, because if we hold on, we will eventually reap.

> I can do all this through him who gives me strength.
>                                         (Philippians 4:13, NIV).

# Wilderness Mentality #4: "I can't help it; I'm just addicted to grumbling, faultfinding and complaining.

*Before you begin, read Chapter 19 in* Battlefield of the Mind.

## Get Ready!

Read 1 Peter 2:19-20. It is not suffering that glorifies God, but

_____

_____

Read 1 Peter 2:21-23.

How did Jesus endure suffering?

_____

_____

_____

_____

Read Ephesians 4:1-2.

To the many people in the world who are trying to find God, what is more important than what we tell them?

_____

_____

_____

_____

Read Psalm 105:17-19; Genesis 39-50.

Why was God eventually able to deliver and promote Joseph who was mistreated by his brothers and unjustly condemned to prison?

_____

_____

_____

Read 1 Corinthians 10:9-11.

How was Joseph different from the Israelites?

_____

_____

_____

What is the message of these passages of Scripture?

_____

_____

_____

What was the difference between the Israelites and Jesus, our example?

_____

_____

_____

What can we see in this contrast?

_____

_____

_____

## Get Set!

Read Philippians 2:14-15.

According to this passage, why are we to do all things without grumbling and faultfinding and complaining?

_____

_____

_____

_____

Read Philippians 4:6.

What does Paul teach us in this verse about how to solve our problems?

_____

_____

_____

When does murmuring, grumbling, faultfinding, and complaining usually occur in our lives?

_____

_____

_____

What does the Word of God teach us to do during these times?

_____

_____

_____

_____

Patience is not the ability to wait, but what?

_____

_____

How can you overcome complaining?

_____

_____

_____

Jesus suffered gloriously! Silently, without complaint, trusting God no matter how things looked, he remained the same in every situation. He did not respond patiently when things were easy and impatiently when they were hard or unjust. (page 208)

## Go to Battle

Many people in the world are trying to find God, and what we show them is much more important than what we tell them. It is, of course, important that we verbally share the gospel, but to do so and negate what we have said with our own behavior is worse than to say nothing. (page 120)

How can remembering how Jesus handled suffering help you?

_____

_____

_____

_____

What are you determined to do differently based on this chapter?

_____

_____

_____

## Remember

Jesus is our example, and we should do what He did.

Do not fret or have any anxiety about anything, but in every circum-stance and in everything, by prayer and petition (definite requests), with thanksgiving, continue to make your wants known to God.

(Philippians 4:6 AMPC).

# Wilderness Mentality #5: "Don't make me wait for anything; I deserve everything immediately."

*Before you begin, read Chapter 20 in* Battlefield of the Mind.

Read James 5:7.

Impatience is the fruit of what?

Why should we learn to be patient while waiting?

_____

_____

_____

What lesson do we need to learn about our life's journey?

_____

_____

_____

Read Romans 12:3.

Why does pride prevent waiting?

_____

_____

_____

A humble person will not display what?

_____

_____

_____

Read John 16:33.

If we get the idea in our heads that everything concerning us and our circumstances and relationships should always be perfect, what are we setting ourselves up for?

_____

_____

How can this be stated another way?

_____

_____

_____

All the mishaps in the world cannot harm us if we will what?

_____

_____

I don't plan for failure, but I do remember that Jesus said that in this world we will have to deal with tribulation and trials and distress and frustration. These things are part of life on this earth—for the believer as well as the unbeliever. But all the mishaps in the world cannot harm us if we will remain in the love of God, displaying the fruit of the Spirit. (page 220)

## Get Set!

Read Colossians 3:12.

How is patience described in this scripture?

_____

_____

Why should we turn to this scripture often?

_____

_____

_____

Look up several versions of the scripture. Write down your favorite version and memorize it.

_____

_____

_____

_____

_____

_____

Read James 1:2-4; Galatians 5:22.

What is patience a fruit of?

_____

_____

_____

According to the New King James Version of James 1, what is the method God uses to bring out patience in us?

_____

_____

_____

Read Numbers 21:4.

According to this scripture, why did the Israelites become impatient, depressed and discouraged?

_____

_____

_____

_____

What will happen if you learn to respond patiently in all kinds of trials?

_____

_____

_____

Read Hebrews 10:36 AMP; 6:12 KJV.

Hebrews 10:36 tells us that without _____ and _____ we will not receive the promises of God. Hebrews 6:12 KJV tells us that it is only through _____ and _____ that we inherit the promises.

## Go to Battle

I really encourage you to work with the Holy Spirit as He develops the fruit of patience in you. The more you resist Him, the longer the process will take. Learn to respond patiently in all kinds of trials, and you will find yourself living a quality of life that is not just endured but enjoyed to the full. (page 222)

Read Proverbs 16:25; John 6:63; Romans 13:14.

Why are there multitudes of unhappy, unfulfilled Christians in the world?

_____

_____

_____

When you are trying to wait on God, why does the devil pound your mind continuously demanding that you "do something"?

_____

_____

_____

Impatience is a sign of pride, and the only answer to pride is what?

_____

_____

Read 1 Peter 5:6.

What does the phrase "lower yourself in your own estimation" mean?

_____

_____

_____

How will you lower yourself in your own estimation as a result of reading this chapter?

_____

_____

_____

What happens when we wait on God and refuse to move in fleshly zeal?

_____

_____

_____

What should you do when you are tempted to become frustrated and impatient?

_____

_____

_____

## Remember

Humility says, "God knows best, and He will not be late!"

Therefore humble yourselves [demote, lower yourselves in your own estimation] under the mighty hand of God, that in due time He may exalt you.

(1 Peter 5:6 AMPC).

# Wilderness Mentality #6: "My behavior may be wrong, but it's not my fault."

*Before you begin, read Chapter 21 in* Battlefield of the Mind.

## Get Ready!

Read Genesis 3:12-13.

Name one major cause for wilderness living.

_____

_____

_____

Read Genesis 16:1-6 NKJV.

Give an example from your own life of blaming others.

_____

_____

_____

Why does Satan work hard on our minds—building strongholds that will prevent us from facing the truth?

_____

_____

_____

Why do we avoid facing the truth about ourselves and our behavior?

_____

_____

_____

Read Numbers 21:5.

Have you ever gone around and around the same mountains in your life? What were your excuses?

_____

_____

_____

_____

Read Numbers 13:1-3, 25-28.

Who plants "ifs" and "buts" in our minds? How should we defeat this tactic?

_____

_____

_____

_____

Name one reason our problems often defeat us.

_____

_____

_____

Like most people, I blamed everything on someone else or some circumstance beyond my control. I thought I was acting badly because I had been abused, but God told me, "Abuse may be the reason you act this way, but don't let it become an excuse to stay this way!"

Satan works hard on our minds—building strongholds that will prevent us from facing truth. The truth will set us free, and he knows it! (page 228)

## Get Set!

Read Psalm 51:1-6.

What does verse 6 mean when it says that God desires truth "in the inner being?"

_____

_____

_____

Read 1 John 1:8-10; Romans 3:20-24.

What must we do to truly repent?

_____

_____

_____

Where is our justification found?

_____

_____

_____

How are you and I made right with God after sinning?

_____

_____

_____

Read John 1:1-5; 8:32.

What is one of the most powerful weapons against the kingdom of darkness? Why?

_____

_____

_____

_____

Jesus said it is truth that sets us free. How is the truth revealed?

_____

_____

## Go to Battle

One of the reasons our problems defeat us is because we think they are bigger than God. That may also be the reason why we have such a hard time facing the truth. We are not sure God can change us, so we hide from ourselves rather than facing ourselves as we really are. (page 230)

Read John 16:12,13; Hebrews 13:5.
    Who is "The Spirit of Truth?"

_____

_____

_____

What is the major facet of His ministry to us? Why?

_____

_____

_____

What has God promised you to help you remember the truth about yourself?

_____

_____

_____

What is left for you to do now that you are on your way out of the wilderness?

_____

_____

_____

_____

## Remember

Ask God to start showing you the truth about yourself. When He does, hang on! It won't be easy, but remember, He has promised, "I will never leave you nor forsake you."

(Hebrews 13:5 NKJV).

Then you will know the truth, and the truth will set you free.

(John 8:32 NIV).

# Wilderness Mentality #7: "My life is so miserable; I feel sorry for myself because my life is so wretched!"

*Before you begin, read Chapter 22 in* Battlefield of the Mind.

## Get Ready!

Read Numbers 14:1-2.

How did the Israelites react to their situation?

_____

_____

_____

What was God's word about such "pity parties?"

_____

_____

_____

What is vitally important to understand about this subject?

_____

_____

_____

_____

Read 1 Thessalonians 5:11.

What does the devil do the minute someone hurts us, the moment we experience disappointment?

_____

_____

_____

What will happen if you listen to the thoughts rushing into your mind during such times?

_____

_____

_____

How is self-pity perverted?

_____

_____

_____

What happens when we take the love of God meant to be given away and turn it in toward ourselves?

_____

_____

_____

What is self-pity? Why is it wrong?

_____

_____

_____

## Get Set!

Read Philippians 2:4.

How do we stay out of self-pity?

_____

_____

How is self-pity supported?

_____

_____

_____

How is self-pity a major trap?

_____

_____

_____

What rare privilege does a Christian have when he experiences disappointment?

_____

_____

_____

We literally exhaust ourselves sometimes trying to gain sympathy. Yes, selfpity is a major trap and one of Satan's favorite tools to keep us in the wilderness. If we are not careful, we can actually become addicted to it. (from page 240)

## Go to Battle

Read Isaiah 43:18-19.

As soon as you feel your emotions starting to rise up, what can you do?

_____

_____

_____

Write a prayer you will use when you feel emotions rising up.

_____

_____

_____

## Remember

A Christian has a rare privilege, because when he experiences disappointment—he can be re-appointed. With God there is always a new beginning available.

> Forget the former things; do not dwell on the past. See, I am doing a new thing! Now it springs up; do you not perceive it? I am making a way in the wilderness and streams in the wasteland.
>
> (Isaiah 43:18-19 NIV).

# Wilderness Mentality #8: "I don't deserve God's blessings because I am not worthy."

*Before you begin, read Chapter 23 in* Battlefield of the Mind.

### Get Ready!

Read Joshua 5:9; Romans 8:17 KJV.

The Lord told Joshua that He had "rolled away" the reproach of Egypt from His people. What does the word "reproach" mean?

_____

_____

_____

God wants to give us grace. What does Satan want to give us?

_____

_____

_____

What does God's rolling away the reproach from us mean?

_____

_____

_____

_____

Although we know we don't deserve God's blessings, why do we receive them anyway? How do we get them?

_____

_____

_____

Read Galatians 4:7.

Are you a son or a slave—an heir or a bond servant?

_____

_____

What is the difference between an heir and a bond servant?

_____

_____

What does experience with the world teach us?

_____

_____

What is the result of this teaching?

_____

_____

We have said that grace is the power of God coming to us, as a free gift from Him, to help us do with ease what we cannot do ourselves. God wants to give us grace, and Satan wants to give us disgrace, which is another word for reproach. (page 248)

## Get Set!

Read Numbers 13:33.

Because of the reproach upon them, what kind of an opinion did the Israelites have of themselves?

_____

_____

How does Satan try to give you a negative opinion of yourself?

_____

_____

How is a poor self-image, an attitude of unworthiness and an "I-don't-deserve-God's-blessings" mentality spread from one generation to the next?

_____

_____

God is willing to give you mercy for your failures if _____. He does not reward the perfect who have no flaws and never make mistakes but _____.

## Go to Battle

Read Hebrews 11:6.

Without _____ you cannot please God. No matter how many _____ you offer, it will not please Him if they were done to _____ His favor.

Read Ephesians 1:4.

According to scripture, what does the Lord want for us?

_____

_____

_____

Read James 1:5; Philippians 1:6.

What does James 1:5 teach us?

_____

_____

_____

If you desire to have a victorious, powerful, positive life, you cannot be negative about yourself. Instead of being negative, what must you do?

_____

_____

In Philippians 1:6, what does Paul say about you?

_____

_____

_____

After reading this chapter, how should you think and speak about yourself?

_____

_____

_____

Which scriptures will help you remember to speak and think about your-self this way?

_____

_____

_____

## Remember

God is willing to give you mercy for your failures if you are willing to receive it.

> Therefore, you are no longer a slave (bond servant) but a son; and if a son, then [it follows that you are] an heir by the aid of God, through Christ.
>
> (Galatians 4:7 AMPC).

# Wilderness Mentality #9: "Why shouldn't I be jealous and envious when everybody else is better off than I am?"

*Before you begin, read Chapter 24 in* Battlefield of the Mind.

## Get Ready!

Read John 21:21-22.

Jealousy, envy and mentally comparing ourselves and our circumstances with others is

_____

_____

Read Proverbs 14:30.

How will envy cause a person to behave?

_____

_____

_____

Define envy and jealousy.

_____

_____

_____

Read Luke 22:24-26.

Why is life in the Kingdom of God usually the direct opposite of the way of the world or the flesh?

_____

_____

_____

Minding (having our mind set on) other people's business, will keep us in the wilderness. Jealousy, envy, and mentally comparing ourselves and our circumstances with others is a wilderness mentality. (page 257)

## Get Set!

Read Galatians 5:26; Proverbs 3:3-4 KJV.

Where does promotion come from for the believer?

_____

_____

God will give us favor with Him and with others if

_____

_____

Read 3 John 2 KJV.

What should you do when you recognize wrong thought patterns beginning to flow into your mind?

_____

_____

_____

Why is it better to be around for the long haul than to be a "shooting star?"

_____

_____

If you have had a mental stronghold for a long time in this area, what should you do? Why? What will be the result?

_____

_____

_____

_____

## Go to Battle!

I found as I grew in the knowledge of who I was in Christ, and not in my works, that I gained freedom in not having to compare myself or anything I did with anyone else. The more I learned to trust God, the more freedom I enjoyed in these areas. I learned that my heavenly Father loves me and will do for me whatever is best—for *me*. What God does for you or for me may not be what He does for someone else, but we must remember what Jesus said to Peter, "Don't be concerned about what I choose to do with someone else—you follow Me!" (page 260)

Write a plan to help you resist comparing yourself to others.

_____

_____

_____

_____

Write down scriptures that will help you remember to do your best with what God has given you as a unique individual.

_____

_____

_____

_____

## Remember

The Bible teaches us that there is no such thing as real peace until we are delivered from the need to compete with others.

> Let us not become conceited, or provoke one another, or be jealous of one another.
>
> (Galatians 5:26 NLT).

# Wilderness Mentality #10: "I'm going to do it my way, or not at all."

*Before you begin, read Chapter 25 in* Battlefield of the Mind.

## Get Ready!

Which wilderness mentality have you worked on so far? What differences have you seen in your thinking and actions.

_____

_____

_____

_____

Read Psalm 78:7-8.

What two mindsets did the Israelites display during their years in the wilderness that caused them to die out there?

_____

_____

_____

What does God demand that we learn? Why?

_____

_____

_____

How are "stubborn" and "rebellious" described? Do either or both of them describe you?

_____

_____

_____

_____

Why is it not enough to reach a certain plateau and think, *I've gone as far as I'm going to go?*

_____

_____

_____

Read 1 Samuel 15:22-23; Romans 5:17; Revelation 1:6 KJV; Ecclesiastes 12:13.

   Why do many of God's children fail to "reign as kings in life"?

_____

_____

_____

How is obedience related to respect and reverence?

_____

_____

_____

If Solomon had so much wisdom, how could he have made so many sad mistakes in his life?

_____

_____

_____

   The Lord demands that we learn to give up our own way and be pliable and moldable in His hands. As long as we are stubborn and rebellious, He can't use us. (page 268)

## Get Set!

Read Romans 5:19 KJV.

Explain how your choice to obey or not to obey not only affects you, but multitudes of others.

_____

_____

_____

Describe obedience as it's discussed in this verse.

_____

_____

_____

Read 2 Corinthians 10:4-5; Isaiah 55:8.

Our thoughts are what get us into trouble quite often. What must we do to avoid this problem?

_____

_____

_____

What should you do if what is in your mind does not agree with God's thoughts (the Bible)?

_____

_____

_____

Satan has launched a war. What is the battlefield?

_____

_____

_____

How will this book assist you to win that war?

_____

_____

_____

## Go to Battle!

What aspect of *Battlefield of the Mind* was most meaningful for you?

_____

_____

_____

Has reading it changed any of the established mindsets you may have had?

_____

_____

_____

Has it helped you in any areas of difficulty and if so, what are they?

_____

_____

_____

_____

What will you do differently as a result of reading *Battlefield of the Mind*?

_____

_____

_____

_____

## Do you have a real relationship with Jesus?

God loves you! He created you to be a special, unique, one-of-a-kind individual, and He has a specific purpose and plan for your life. And through a personal relationship with your Creator—God—you can discover a way of life that will truly satisfy your soul.

No matter who you are, what you've done, or where you are in your life right now, God's love and grace are greater than your sin—your mistakes. Jesus willingly gave His life so you can receive forgiveness from God and have new life in Him. He's just waiting for you to invite Him to be your Savior and Lord.

If you are ready to commit your life to Jesus and follow Him, all you have to do is ask Him to forgive your sins and give you a fresh start in the life you are meant to live. Begin by praying this prayer...

*Lord Jesus, thank You for giving Your life for me and forgiving me of my sins so I can have a personal relationship with You. I am sincerely sorry for the mistakes I've made, and I know I need You to help me live right.*

*Your Word says in Romans 10:9, "If you declare with your mouth, 'Jesus is Lord,' and believe in your heart that God raised him from the dead, you will be saved" (NIV). I believe You are the Son of God and confess You as my Savior and Lord. Take me just as I am, and work in my heart, making me the person You want me to be. I want to live for You, Jesus, and I am so grateful that You are giving me a fresh start in my new life with You today.*

*I love You, Jesus!*

It's so amazing to know that God loves us so much! He wants to have a deep, intimate relationship with us that grows every day as we spend time with Him in prayer and Bible study. And we want to encourage you in your new life in Christ.

Please visit joycemeyer.org/salvation to request Joyce's book *A New Way of Living*, which is our gift to you. We also have other free resources online to help you make progress in pursuing everything God has for you.

Congratulations on your fresh start in your life in Christ! We hope to hear from you soon.

**Joyce Meyer Ministries**
P.O. Box 655
Fenton, MO 63026
USA
(636) 349-0303

**Joyce Meyer Ministries—Canada**
P.O. Box 7700
Vancouver, BC V6B 4E2
Canada
(800) 868-1002

**Joyce Meyer Ministries—Australia**
Locked Bag 77
Mansfield Delivery Centre
Queensland 4122
Australia
(07) 3349 1200

**Joyce Meyer Ministries—England**
P.O. Box 1549
Windsor SL4 1GT
United Kingdom
01753 831102

**Joyce Meyer Ministries—South Africa**
P.O. Box 5
Cape Town 8000
South Africa
(27) 21-701-1056

*New Day, New You*
*Overload*
*The Penny*
*Perfect Love* (previously published as *God Is Not Mad at You*)*
*The Power of Being Positive*
*The Power of Being Thankful*
*The Power of Determination*
*The Power of Forgiveness*
*The Power of Simple Prayer*
*Power Thoughts*
*Power Thoughts Devotional*
*Reduce Me to Love*
*The Secret Power of Speaking God's Word*
*The Secrets of Spiritual Power*
*The Secret to True Happiness*
*Seven Things That Steal Your Joy*
*Start Your New Life Today*
*Starting Your Day Right*
*Straight Talk*
*Teenagers Are People Too!*
*Trusting God Day by Day*
*The Word, the Name, the Blood*
*Woman to Woman*
*You Can Begin Again*

JOYCE MEYER SPANISH TITLES

*Belleza en Lugar de Cenizas (Beauty for Ashes)*
*Buena Salud, Buena Vida (Good Health, Good Life)*
*Cambia Tus Palabras, Cambia Tu Vida (Change Your Words, Change Your Life)*
*El Campo de Batalla de la Mente (Battlefield of the Mind)*
*Como Formar Buenos Habitos y Romper Malos Habitos (Making Good Habits, Breaking Bad Habits)*
*La Conexión de la Mente (The Mind Connection)*
*Dios No Está Enojado Contigo (God Is Not Mad at You)*
*La Dosis de Aprobación (The Approval Fix)*
*Empezando Tu Día Bien (Starting Your Day Right)*
*Hazte Un Favor a Ti Mismo…Perdona (Do Yourself a Favor…Forgive)*
*Madre Segura de sí Misma (The Confident Mom)*
*Pensamientos de Poder (Power Thoughts)*
*Sobrecarga (Overload)**
*Termina Bien tu Día (Ending Your Day Right)*
*Usted Puede Comenzar de Nuevo (You Can Begin Again)*
*Viva Valientemente (Living Courageously)*
*Study Guide available for this title

BOOKS BY DAVE MEYER

*Life Lines*

JOYCE MEYER is one of the world's leading practical Bible teachers. A *New York Times* bestselling author, Joyce's books have helped millions of people find hope and restoration through Jesus Christ. Joyce's programs, *Enjoying Everyday Life* and *Everyday Answers with Joyce Meyer,* air around the world on television, radio, and the Internet. Through Joyce Meyer Ministries, Joyce teaches internationally on a number of topics with a particular focus on how the Word of God applies to our everyday lives. Her candid communication style allows her to share openly and practically about her experiences so others can apply what she has learned to their lives.

Joyce has authored more than 100 books, which have been translated into more than 100 languages, and over 65 million of her books have been distributed worldwide. Bestsellers include *Power Thoughts*; *The Confident Woman*; *Look Great, Feel Great*; *Starting Your Day Right*; *Ending Your Day Right*; *Approval Addiction*; *How to Hear from God*; *Beauty for Ashes*; and *Battlefield of the Mind*.

Joyce's passion to help hurting people is foundational to the vision of Hand of Hope, the missions arm of Joyce Meyer Ministries. Hand of Hope provides worldwide humanitarian outreaches such as feeding programs, medical care, orphanages, disaster response, human trafficking intervention and rehabilitation, and much more—always sharing the love and Gospel of Christ.

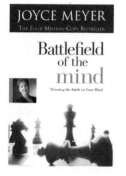
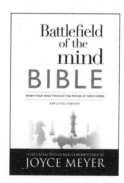

NOTES

Notes